100 INTERVIEW QUESTIONS TO CRACK A SCHOOL PRINCIPAL'S JOB

DR DHEERAJ MEHROTRA

Contents

Preface

A principal's appointment marks the move from teaching and administration to leading a school community. This position requires vision, leadership, education, and interpersonal skills. In "100 Interview Questions To Crack a School Principal's Job," aspiring principals are given the skills and insights they need to succeed in the demanding interview process.

Principal interviews require a strong understanding of educational theories, dedication to establishing a positive school culture, and the capacity to lead with integrity and vision. This book has 100 well-selected interview questions. Each question thoroughly explains how to respond with competence, confidence, and passion for educational leadership.

We know that becoming a school principal is complex and uncertain. With careful preparation and a clear awareness of interviewers' expectations, aspiring principals can confidently present themselves as the ideal candidates for this crucial post. This book will help you shine in your interview and land your desired job by lending you knowledge and insights.

Remember that becoming a school principal is a calling, not a job. It's an opportunity to shape education, motivate instructors, and change students' lives. This book should inspire you to take this road with confidence, clarity, and a dedication to education.

Your first step toward becoming a school principal. Best of luck with your interview and leadership career.

Dr. Dheeraj Mehrotra
July 2024
   www.authordheerajmehrotra.com

"Success in an interview comes not just from answering questions, but from authentically showcasing your passion, vision, and ability to lead."

PREFACE

CHAPTER ONE

Getting to go!

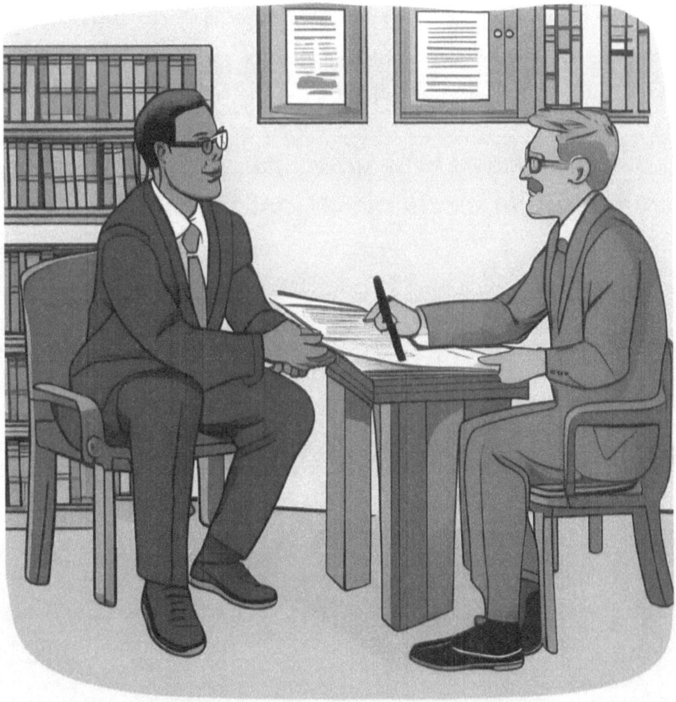

"Remember, an interview is not an interrogation but a conversation. Engage, connect, and be your authentic self."

Vision & Leadership

1. **What do you see for our school?**

- *Answer:* My objective is to foster an inclusive, safe, and innovative learning environment in which all students are motivated to reach their full potential.

2. **How would you characterize effective leadership in a school setting?**

- *Answer:* Effective leadership entails establishing a clear vision, encouraging teamwork among staff, involving the community, and responding to the needs of kids and teachers.

3. **Could you give me an example of how you led a successful initiative at your former school?**

- *Answer:* At my former school, I spearheaded

a technology integration effort that boosted student engagement and academic performance by incorporating digital tools into the curriculum.

Instructional Leadership

4. **How do you keep up with educational developments and best practices?**

- *Answer:* To stay current, I attend professional development courses, read educational publications, participate in online forums, and network with other educators.

5. **What strategies do you employ to boost student achievement?**

- *Answer:* My primary focus is on data-driven decision-making, differentiated instruction, teacher professional development, and fostering a supportive and motivating school culture.

6. **How do you ensure that the curriculum addresses the requirements of all students?**

- *Answer:* I review and revise the curriculum regularly, considering comments from teachers, students, and parents while maintaining alignment with state standards and our children's diverse needs.

School Culture and Environment

7. **How would you define the ideal school culture?**

- *Answer:* An ideal school culture is one in which children feel safe and appreciated, teachers are motivated and encouraged, and the entire school community works together to achieve shared goals.

8. **What steps do you take to ensure a positive school climate?**

- *Answer:* I implement programs that promote respect and diversity, set clear behavioural expectations, and provide student and staff appreciation chances.

9. **How do you resolve disagreements among students or staff?**

- *Answer:* I resolve problems promptly and fairly, fostering open communication, mediation, and collaborative solutions that respect all parties involved.

"Approach each interview with curiosity and openness;
it's an opportunity to learn about the organization and

yourself."

Student and Staff Management

10. **How do you encourage professional development for teachers?**

- *Answer:* I offer opportunities for continual training, encourage peer observations and mentorship, and provide funding for teachers to attend conferences and seminars.

11. **What is your method for evaluating teacher performance?**

- *Answer:* I use classroom observations, student accomplishment statistics, and self-reflections to provide constructive criticism and support for teachers' professional development.

12. **How do you engage parents in the educational process?**

- *Answer:* I promote open communication, create volunteer opportunities, hold regular parent-teacher meetings, and keep parents up to date on school activities and student progress.

Operations Management

13. **How do you handle the school's budget?**

- *Answer:* I prioritize spending based on school goals, maintain transparency, involve key stakeholders in budgeting choices, and check financial data regularly to stay within budget.

14. **What precautions do you take to protect your kids' and staff's safety and security?**

- *Answer:* I implement detailed safety plans, run frequent drills, ensure the school has the required security measures, and promote a culture of awareness and preparedness.

15. **How do you deal with the challenges of

*limited resources?***

- *Answer:* I prioritize priorities, explore alternate financing sources such as grants, and use limited resources best through careful planning and collaboration.

Community Engagement

16. **How do you develop partnerships with community partners?**

- *Answer:* I regularly interact with local businesses, non-profits, and community leaders to identify opportunities for collaboration that benefit our students and school programs.

17. **What role do you envision the school playing in the local community?**

- *Answer:* The school should serve as a community hub, providing educational and recreational opportunities while instilling a *shared responsibility for student achievement.*

*18. **How do you handle criticism or nasty comments from your community?***

*- *Answer:* I actively listen, address concerns transparently, and collaborate to create solutions consistent with the school's mission and community requirements.*

"Interviews are not just about answering questions;
they're about demonstrating your unique value
proposition."

Student Support and Well-Being

19. **How do you help pupils with specific needs?**

- *Answer:* I guarantee that individualized education plans (IEPs) are implemented, staff have access to the tools and training required, and an inclusive atmosphere is created to accommodate all learners.

20. **What is your strategy for addressing student mental health?**

- *Answer:* I implement programs that raise mental health awareness, provide counselling services, and foster a caring school culture that promotes student well-being.

21. **How do you deal with situations of bullying?**

- *Answer:* I have a zero-tolerance policy, educate people about the effects of bullying, ensure rapid action, and help both victims and perpetrators resolve underlying issues.

Technology and Innovation

22. **How do you integrate technology in the classroom?**

- *Answer:* I support educational technology by training teachers, providing access to digital tools, and encouraging the use of technology to improve learning and engagement.

23. **Are you experts with remote or hybrid learning models?**

- *Answer:* I have developed remote and hybrid learning models, guaranteeing that students have access to high-quality education regardless of their location and assisting teachers in adapting to these new forms.

24. **How do you prepare pupils for future job opportunities?**

- *Answer:* I prioritize the development of critical thinking, problem-solving, and digital literacy skills, as well as opportunities for career exploration and hands-on experience.

Future Vision

25. **Where do you envision the school in five years?**

- *Answer:* I see our school as a leader in

academic excellence and creativity, with a strong sense of community and a dedication to educating students for success in an ever-changing world.

26. **What initiatives would you take to attain this vision?**

- *Answer:* I would prioritize improving curriculum and instruction, boosting professional development, cultivating community collaborations, and harnessing technology to enhance individualized learning.

Additional Questions:

27. **How do you combine administrative responsibilities while remaining accessible and approachable to students and staff?**

- *Answer:* I prioritize time management, assign responsibilities as needed, and make a concerted effort to be present in classrooms and common spaces to interact with students and staff.

28. **How do you handle stress and maintain a healthy work-life balance?**

- *Answer:* I manage stress and maintain a healthy work-life balance by practising self-care, setting boundaries, prioritizing tasks, and seeking support from colleagues and mentors.

29. **Can you recount an instance when you had to make a difficult decision?**

- *Response:* I once had to relocate a valued teacher to a different grade level due to student needs. I talked openly with everyone involved and offered assistance to achieve a smooth transition.

30. **How do you encourage innovation and originality among your employees?**

- *Answer:* I promote experimentation, offer opportunities for professional development, recognize and reward innovative methods, and foster a culture that values and supports new ideas.

"Think of an interview as a performance: prepare, rehearse, and deliver confidently."

31. **How does data influence your decision-making process?**

- *Answer:* Data is critical for identifying areas for improvement, establishing goals, *measuring progress, and making educated decisions to improve student outcomes and school performance.*

32. **How do you address a situation where a teacher does not fulfil performance standards?**

- *Answer:* I swiftly address the issue using a constructive feedback method, provide help and resources for improvement, and track progress to ensure positive improvements are made.

33. **What strategies do you utilize to foster a strong school community?**

- *Answer:* I encourage open communication, collaborative opportunities, success recognition, and a sense of belonging among students, staff, and parents.

34. **How do you promote equity and inclusivity in your school?**

- *Answer:* I adopt policies and practices that encourage diversity, provide professional development in cultural competency, and *guarantee that all students can access the resources and assistance required to succeed.*

*35. **How do you handle budget cuts?***

*- *Answer:* I prioritize critical programs, seek alternate financing sources, include stakeholders in decision-making, and look for innovative ways to sustain quality education with limited resources.*

*36. **How do you deal with resistance to change from staff or parents?***

*- *Answer:* I address issues by open communication, engage stakeholders in the change process, provide a clear reason and advantages, and provide assistance to smooth the transition.*

*37. **How do extracurricular activities fit into your vision for the school?***

*- *Answer:* Extracurricular activities are important for kids' overall development because they allow them to explore their interests, develop their abilities, and foster*

community and school pride.

*38. **How do you encourage student leadership and voice in the school?***

*- *Answer:* I provide outlets for student feedback, encourage participation in decision-making processes, and support student-led initiatives and leadership development programs.*

*39. **How do you meet the needs of English Language Learners (ELLs)?***

*- *Answer:* I offer focused assistance through specialized programs, professional development for teachers, and tools that promote language acquisition and cultural inclusion.*

*40. **How do you approach curriculum development?***

*- *Answer:* I guarantee that the curriculum is linked with standards, incorporates best practices, and is responsive to our students' needs while encouraging creativity and critical*

thinking.

"An interview is a two-way street; it's as much about
you assessing the role as it is about them assessing you."

41. **How do you address parental complaints or concerns?**

- *Answer:* I listen attentively, handle problems swiftly and fairly, keep open communication, and work. I also tend to Collaborate to develop solutions that benefit students and the school community.

42. **What are your priorities for school improvement?**

- *Answer:* My top priorities include increasing student achievement, boosting teacher effectiveness, creating a great school climate, and developing strong community partnerships.

43. **How do you ensure successful communication in the school?**

- *Answer:* I communicate using a variety of channels, including newsletters, meetings, emails, and social media, and I make sure that all conversations are transparent and open.

44. **How do you approach professional learning communities (PLCs)?**

- *Answer:* I help PLCs by giving them time, resources, and advice, fostering cooperation, data-driven conversations, and focusing on continual development.

45. **How do you deal with underperforming students?**

- *Answer:* I discover the underlying causes of underperformance, offer focused interventions and support, and collaborate with teachers and parents to develop personalized improvement plans, which include Remedials and Home Visits.

46. **What experience do you have with special education programs?**

- *Answer:* I have managed special education programs, ensuring regulatory compliance, assisting instructors, and fighting for the needs and rights of kids with disabilities. Since we are an inclusive school, as per the NEP, we follow the guidelines and implement the policies as per the board's circulars.

47. **How do you encourage continuous improvement among your employees?**

- *Answer:* I foster a culture of reflection and growth, offer professional development opportunities, and promote collaboration and the exchange of best practices.

48. **How do you handle issues of academic integrity and cheating?**

- *Answer:* I develop clear standards, educate students and staff about academic integrity, monitor for violations, and enforce punishments like having two rounds of the field or making them write "I am sorry for 100 times", avoiding Physical Punishments while creating an honest and responsible culture.

49. **What role does social-emotional learning

*(SEL) play at your school?***

- *Answer:* SEL is built into our approach, including programs and activities that promote kids' emotional well-being, resilience, and interpersonal skills.

50. **How do you handle the school's facilities and resources?**

- *Answer:* I keep facilities in good condition, use resources efficiently, emphasize safety and accessibility, and prepare for future requirements and enhancements.

"Interviews are about storytelling—telling your story in a way that aligns with the organization's vision and values."

51. **How do you deal with absence and truancy?**

- *Answer:* I address absenteeism by

intervening early, communicating with parents, providing help for underlying difficulties, and, if required, involving community resources.

52. **How do you foster a growth mentality in students and staff?**

- *Answer:* I encourage focusing on effort and improvement, reward progress, give constructive comments, and demonstrate a growth mindset through my actions and attitudes.

53. **How do you approach hiring and keeping quality teachers?**

- *Answer:* I recruit exceptional educators, foster a supportive and collaborative work atmosphere, provide professional development opportunities, and recognize and reward excellence. I also use professional social media platforms like LinkedIn to hire applicants and connect with outsourced HR Agencies.

54. **How do you make sure the school satisfies state and federal education standards?**

- *Answer:* I stay current on regulations, ensure curriculum alignment, monitor compliance, and provide training and resources to satisfy standards. Following SQAA as a part of school quality assessment by respective boards.

55. **What is your perspective on standardized testing?**

- *Answer:* Standardized testing is an effective tool for measuring certain aspects of student accomplishment. However, it should be used with other assessment forms to create a complete picture of student learning.

56. **How do you include instructors' feedback in your decision-making process?**

- *Answer:* I establish avenues for regular feedback, include teachers in committees and planning, and appreciate their perspectives and experience in establishing school policies and procedures.

57. **What experience do you have in grant writing and fundraising?**

- *Answer:* I've successfully written grants and led fundraising campaigns to acquire more funding for programs, technology, and school enhancements.

58. **How do you ensure that extracurricular activities are inclusive and diverse?**

- *Answer:* I offer a variety of activities that reflect all students' interests and experiences, guarantee equal access, and encourage involvement from diverse groups.

59. **How do you handle disciplinary issues?**

- *Answer:* I use fair and consistent disciplinary procedures, prioritize restorative practices, and collaborate with students, parents, and staff to address root causes and promote positive behaviour.

60. **How do you foster a culture of academic excellence?**

- *Answer:* I set high standards, provide help

and resources, acknowledge and celebrate accomplishments, and foster a climate that values and encourages academic success. I also implement KAIZEN as a practice philosophy.

"Every interview is a step towards your career goals; treat each one as an opportunity to learn and grow."

*61. **How do you support new teachers?***

- *Answer:* I offer a comprehensive induction program, assign mentors, give continuous professional development, and foster a supportive network for incoming teachers.

62. **How do you engage pupils in their learning?**

- *Answer:* I support active learning, use technology, differentiate instruction, and foster a lively and inclusive classroom climate that encourages kids to participate. We can also engage them through the integration of technology and AI tools.

63. **How do you manage budget overruns?**

- *Answer:* I closely monitor expenditures, identify and address sources of overruns, and make required changes while being transparent and accountable.

64. **What role do you believe parents should take in their children's education?**

- *Answer:* Parents are essential partners in

education, and I promote their participation through regular contact, volunteering, decision-making, and support for learning at home.

65. **How do you deal with the problems of a diverse student population?**

- *Answer:* I encourage cultural competence, ensure inclusive policies and procedures, support varied needs, and appreciate diversity's value to our school community.

66. **What experience do you have with curriculum mapping?**

- *Answer:* I've led curriculum mapping initiatives to guarantee standards alignment, grade-level coherence, and a well-rounded educational program.

67. **How do you encourage ethical behaviour among students and staff?**

- *Answer:* I demonstrate ethical behaviour, develop clear norms of conduct, educate others on ethical concerns, and foster an environment *that values honesty and respect.*

68. **What are your top priorities for establishing a new program or initiative?**

- *Answer:* *My top priorities are ensuring alignment with school goals, securing necessary resources, involving stakeholders in planning, and monitoring and evaluating the program's effects.*

69. **How do you maintain data privacy and security?**

- *Answer:* *I develop strong data privacy rules, assure regulatory compliance, train employees, and use secure systems to protect sensitive information.*

70. **How do you promote innovation in teaching and learning?**

- *Answer:* *I encourage experimentation with new methods, give professional development on innovative practices, and foster an environment that promotes creativity and risk-taking.*

"An interview is the bridge between where you are and where you want to be; cross it with preparation and poise."

71. **How do you approach managing school facilities?**

- *Answer:* I ensure that facilities are safe, clean, and conducive to learning, plan *maintenance and upgrades, and work with the community to maintain a high-quality learning environment.*

72. **How do you meet the needs of exceptional and talented students?**

- *Answer:* I offer differentiated education, advanced courses, enrichment activities, and opportunities for gifted students to pursue their passions and abilities.

73. **How do you foster trust among students, staff, and parents?**

- *Answer:* I establish trust through transparency, consistency, active listening, keeping promises, and fostering an open and respectful school culture.

74. **What is your experience with the school accreditation process?**

- *Answer:* I have led schools through accreditation processes, ensuring standard compliance, preparing documentation, and facilitating accreditor visits.

75. **How do you manage competing demands on your time?**

- *Answer:* I prioritize tasks based on urgency and importance, delegate when necessary, keep a flexible schedule, and use effective time management strategies to balance demands.

76. **What is your strategy for dealing with low staff morale?**

- *Answer:* I address the underlying reasons for low morale, offer support and appreciation, foster a positive and inclusive atmosphere, and provide chances for employees to express their problems and make suggestions.

77. **How do you promote the professional development of your administrative team?**

- *Answer:* I promote the growth of my administrative team by providing mentorship, professional development opportunities, regular feedback, and leadership development programs.

78. **What is your experience with blended learning?**

- *Answer:* I've used blended learning approaches that combine traditional education with online components to increase flexibility and improve student engagement and learning outcomes.

79. **How do you deal with unfavourable publicity regarding the school?**

- *Answer:* I proactively respond to negative news by speaking honestly with stakeholders, providing accurate information, and addressing underlying issues.

80. **What strategies do you employ to maintain good classroom management?**

- *Answer:* I train teachers on classroom management strategies, assist them in setting clear standards, and foster a sound and courteous classroom atmosphere.

"In an interview, your authenticity, confidence, and ability to connect are as important as the answers you give."

81. **How do you deal with objections to new initiatives?**

- *Answer:* I involve stakeholders in planning,

express the benefits clearly, offer help during implementation, and respond to concerns and resistance with empathy and understanding.

82. **How do you ensure that your school is inclusive and accessible to all students?**

- *Answer:* I develop policies and practices that promote diversity, maintain physical accessibility, make necessary accommodations, and foster a welcoming atmosphere for all students.

83. **How do you approach student assessment?**

- *Answer:* I employ various assessment methods, including formative and summative assessments, to provide a comprehensive view of student learning. I also ensure that assessments are fair and consistent with learning objectives.

84. **How do you manage staff turnover?**

- *Answer:* I investigate the causes of turnover, enhance retention techniques, offer assistance *throughout transitions, and maintain a robust recruitment process to attract and retain great employees.*

85. **What is your experience with restorative justice?**

- *Answer:* I've employed restorative justice approaches to resolve disagreements, promote responsibility, and foster a healthy school culture centred on repairing harm and rebuilding relationships.

86. **How do you foster a culture of collaboration among employees?**

- *Answer:* I foster teamwork, encourage open communication, provide collaborative planning time, and recognize and reward cooperative accomplishments.

87. **What role do you envision technology playing in education?**

- *Answer:* Technology is critical in improving learning, providing access to resources, enabling tailored instruction, and preparing *students for a digital future.*

*88. **How do you respond to the needs of pupils from low-income families?***

*- *Answer:* I give focused support, assure access to resources and programs, engage community partners, and foster an inclusive environment that promotes student achievement.*

*89. **How do you approach professional development for non-teaching staff?***

*- *Answer:* I offer chances for growth and training to all staff, recognizing their critical role in advancing the school's purpose and establishing a positive learning environment.*

*90. **How do you communicate the school's mission and values?***

*- *Answer:* I consistently convey the mission and values, incorporate them into decision-making and daily operations, and ensure all stakeholders understand and support them.*

"An interview is not just a test of knowledge, but a chance to showcase your passion, vision, and readiness for the role."

91. **How do you address legal issues that emerge at school?**

- *Answer:* I engage with legal experts, ensure

compliance with laws and regulations, train staff, and respond to issues promptly and suitably.

92. **What is your experience with project-based learning?**

- *Answer:* I've used project-based learning to engage students in real-world challenges, develop critical thinking and teamwork, and increase the relevance of their education.

93. **How do you support the arts at your school?**

- *Answer:* I ensure that arts programs are well-funded and integrated into the curriculum, that students can participate, and that the arts are celebrated in education.

94. **What is your strategy for developing a solid school board relationship?**

- *Answer:* I maintain open communication, provide regular updates, engage the board in strategic planning, and work together to promote the school's mission and goals.

95. **How do you address the issues of rural and urban education?**

- *Answer:* I customize tactics to fit the specific needs of rural or urban areas, engage the community, close resource gaps, and create possibilities for student success.

96. **How do you address contentious issues or policies at the school?**

- *Answer:* I address contentious topics with transparency, solicit stakeholder feedback, communicate clearly and consistently, and make choices in the best interests of kids and the school community.

97. **What is your experience in early childhood education?**

- *Answer:* I have helped early childhood education programs by guaranteeing high-quality content, professional development for instructors, and a nurturing environment that encourages early learning and development.

98. **How do you keep school policies fair and equitable?**

- *Answer:* I examine policies regularly, solicit feedback from various stakeholders, ensure adherence to laws and best practices, and make changes to enhance fairness and equity.

99. **How do you handle emergencies or crises?**

- *Answer:* I have a detailed emergency plan, organize frequent drills, communicate effectively with stakeholders, and assist individuals affected during and after a crisis.

100. **How do you recognize and publicize the accomplishments of students and staff?**

- *Answer:* I acknowledge accomplishments through awards, assemblies, newsletters, and social media, and I foster an environment where success is honoured and everyone feels valued and appreciated.

"Interviews are conversations where skills meet opportunities, and first impressions become lasting decisions."

CHAPTER TWO

Final Tips & Strategies

"An interview is not just a test of knowledge, but a showcase of character, resilience, and the ability to inspire."

Interview Portfolio Preparation

An interview portfolio is a critical resource demonstrating your qualifications, accomplishments, and vision for the role of school principal. Here is a method for crafting an impactful presentation:

*1. **Organize Your Documents**: Compile a resume, cover letter, transcripts, certifications, and letters of recommendation. Arrange them logically, with the most critical documents at the front.*

*2. **Emphasize Your Accomplishments**: Provide concrete examples to illustrate your achievements. Incorporate data and metrics, including the successful implementation of programs, improvements in test scores, and any awards or recognitions you have received.*

*3. **Include a Statement of Leadership Philosophy**: Clearly express your educational philosophy and leadership style. Your vision for the school and the strategies you intend to employ to realize it should be reflected in this statement.*

4. **Provide Examples of Successful Projects**: Include case studies or project summaries that emphasize your leadership skills and problem-solving abilities. Concentrate on initiatives that had a substantial positive influence on the school community.

5. **Visual Aids**: Employ photographs, diagrams, and charts to elucidate your arguments. Visual assets can enhance the engagement and ease of navigation of your portfolio.

6. **Digital Version**: Develop a digital version of your portfolio that can be accessed on a laptop or tablet. This demonstrates your technological proficiency and readiness to adapt to any interview format.

"Success in an interview comes not just from answering questions, but from authentically showcasing your passion, vision, and ability to lead."

Dressing for Success

Your physical appearance has the potential to leave a lasting impression. Dressing appropriately for an interview is essential for conveying confidence and professionalism:

*1. **Research the Dress Code**: Familiarize yourself with the dress code of the school or district. When uncertain, choose professional business attire.*

*2. **Select Conservative Colors**: Opt for neutral hues such as black, navy, or grey. Professionalism and solemnity are conveyed through these colours.*

*3. **Ensure a Comfortable Fit**: Your clothing should be comfortable and well-fitted. Please refrain from wearing excessively tight or unfastened clothing, which may cause distractions.*

*4. **Pay Attention to Grooming**: Ensure that your hair is orderly; facial hair should be appropriately groomed. It is recommended that nails be kept clean and trimmed and jewellery be kept minimal and tasteful.*

*5. **Reduce Fragrances**: Use perfumes or colognes in moderation. Strong fragrances can* *be overwhelming, causing allergic reactions.*

*6. **Test Your Outfit**: Before the interview, wear your selected attire for a few hours to guarantee comfort and self-assurance.*

Post-Interview Follow-Up

The benefits of following up after an interview are showing professionalism and reinforcing your interest in the position. The following is an effective method for achieving this:

1. **Send a Thank-You Note**: Within 24 hours of the interview, send a thank-you email. Reiterate your enthusiasm for the position, express gratitude for the opportunity, and briefly mention a specific topic that was discussed.

2. **Handwritten Notes**: If appropriate, consider sending a handwritten thank-you note in addition to that email. It can help one distinguish oneself and provide a personal flourish.

3. **Follow Up on Timelines**: If the interviewers mentioned a decision timeline, wait until after that period to follow up. If no timetable was provided, a civil inquiry should be made after one to two weeks.

4. **Contemplate the Interview**: Utilize this opportunity to assess your performance. Determine the areas in which you flourished and those in which you can develop.

5. **Maintain Professionalism**: Maintaining professionalism in all communications, regardless of the outcome, is imperative. If you cannot obtain the position, express gratitude for the opportunity and indicate your interest in being considered for future positions.

Common Mistakes to Avoid

Your interview performance can be substantially improved by avoiding common hazards. The following are significant hazards that should be observed:

*1. **Unpreparedness**: The absence of preparation is readily apparent. Conduct research on the institution, comprehend its opportunities and obstacles, and be prepared to articulate the extent to which your qualifications and experiences are compatible.*

*2. **Over-Talking or Under-Talking**: Strive to balance your responses harmoniously.*

Under-talking can give the impression that you are unprepared or disinterested while over-talking can make you appear unfocused.

*3. **Negativity**: It is advisable to refrain from discussing past employers or colleagues in a negative light. It has the potential to impact your attitude and professionalism negatively.*

*4. **Vague Responses**: Please provide detailed responses. Clearly articulate your thoughts and substantiate your claims with examples.*

*5. **Inadequate Questions**: Develop insightful inquiries to pose to the interviewers. This will demonstrate your enthusiasm for the position and assist you in determining whether the institution is a suitable match for you.*

*6. **Ignoring Non-Verbal Cues**: Observing the interviewer's body language and yourself is essential. Sit up erect, maintain eye contact, and refrain from fidgeting.*

Adhering to these final strategies and recommendations can establish you as a well-prepared and formidable candidate, enhancing your likelihood of obtaining your desired school principal position.

25 Ways to Make a Good First Impression at an Interview

*1. **Research the Company**: Show that you know a lot about the company's purpose, values, most recent projects, and position in the industry—answer in a way that helps them reach their goals.*

*2. **Understand the Role**: Make sure you fully understand the job's duties and needs. Show why your skills and experience make you the best person for the job.*

3. Get ready for a strong start: Start with an engaging personal introduction about your applicable experience and why you're excited about the job.

*4. **Dress Appropriately**: Wear professional and appropriate clothes for the job. A clean look shows that you take the job seriously and respect it.*

*5. **Bring a Portfolio**: Make sure you have a well-organized portfolio with your resume, work samples, and references with you. This physical proof can help prove your skills.*

*6. **Ask Insightful Questions**: Consider what you want to know about the company's culture, problems, and goals. This shows that you are interested and can think critically.*

*7. **Be On Time**: Get there on time, ideally 10 to 15 minutes early. Being on time shows you can be trusted and value the interviewer's time.*

*8. **Work on active listening**: Pay close attention to the interviewer's comments and questions. Think about what you say, and don't interrupt.*

*9. **Show Off Your Soft Skills**: Show off your people skills, like how well you can communicate, work with others, and solve problems by providing evidence from your life.*

10. Make eye contact, sit up straight, and speak adequately to show you are sure of yourself. Employers like people who are confident without being cocky.

*11. **Use the STAR Method**: To give clear and concise answers to* *behavioural questions, use the STAR method (Situation, Task, Action, Result) to organize your replies.*

12. Make your unique selling points stand out: Figure out what differentiates you from other applicants, and stress these points during the interview.

*13. **Follow Up with Enthusiasm**: After the interview, send a personalized thank-you email or note expressing your appreciation for the opportunity and your interest in the job.*

*14. **Show Adaptability**: You can learn quickly and adjust to new conditions. Give examples of times when you dealt with change well.*

*15. **Be Honest**: When asked a question, tell the truth. Say you're ready to learn and admit you don't know something.*

*16. **Relate Your Experience to the Job**: Make clear links between what you've done in the past and what the job requires. This helps the interviewer determine whether you fit the job well.*

17. **Show How Much You Love the Industry**: Show that you're genuinely interested and passionate about the business by talking about new ideas and trends that interest you.

18. **Show Problem-Solving Skills**: Give examples of how you've solved problems well in past jobs. This shows that you can deal with problems.

19. **Get Ready for Common Questions**: Think about and practice answering common interview questions. Getting ready helps you stay relaxed and concentrate.

20. **Build Rapport**: Get to know the speaker by finding things you have in common. This will make the interview feel less formal and more like a discussion.

21. **Bring Your Energy**: Be happy and full of energy. Being excited can spread and affect the interviewer that lasts.

22. **Showcase Continuous Learning**: Show how committed you

are to growing as a person and worker. List any courses, certifications, or learning events you've had recently.

23. Give Quantifiable Achievements: Talk about specific, measurable things you did well in your previous jobs to show how much of an effect you had and how successful you were.

*24. **Use Positive Body Language**: Keep your body language open and positive throughout the conversation. Do not fidget, and keep a cool attitude.*

*25. **Write a closing sentence**: Say something strong at the end of the interview that summarizes why you're the best person for the job and how excited you are to join the team.*

"The true objective of education is not merely to
transfer knowledge but to ignite a passion for learning,
foster critical thinking, and cultivate a sense of
responsibility and empathy. It aims to prepare individuals
to contribute positively to society and navigate the
complexities of life with wisdom and integrity."

CHAPTER THREE

Top 10 Important Online Courses for School Principals

1.   **Educational Leadership and Management**
-   **Platform:** Coursera (University of Illinois)
- **Description:** This course covers essential leadership theories, strategic planning, and effective management practices crucial for school principals.

2. **School Administration and Supervision**
- **Platform:** edX (Harvard University)
- **Description:** Focuses on the roles and responsibilities of school administrators, including supervision techniques, decision-

making processes, and policy implementation.

*3.   **Data-Driven   Decision-Making   in Education***
*-   **Platform:**   Coursera   (University   of California, Irvine)*
*- **Description:** Teaches how to use data to inform decision-making processes, improve student   outcomes,   and   enhance   school performance.*

*4. **Financial Management in Schools***
*-   **Platform:**   FutureLearn   (Chartered College of Teaching)*
*- **Description:** Covers budgeting, financial planning, resource allocation, and financial oversight specific to the educational sector.*

*5. **Educational Technology Leadership***
*-   **Platform:**   Coursera   (University   of Michigan)*
*Description:** This course explores integrating technology in education, using digital tools for teaching   and   learning,   and   leading   a technology-driven school environment.*

*6.   **Conflict   Resolution   in   Educational Settings***
*- **Platform:** edX (University of London)*

- **Description:** Provides strategies for resolving conflicts among students, staff, and parents, fostering a collaborative and peaceful school environment.

7. **Strategic Leadership in Education**
- **Platform:** Coursera (University of Minnesota)
- **Description:** Focuses on developing strategic leadership skills, vision creation, and implementing change within educational institutions.

8. **Inclusive Leadership in Education**
- **Platform:** FutureLearn (Deakin University)
- **Description:** Addresses inclusive practices, equity in education, and strategies for supporting diverse student populations.

9. **Human Resource Management for School Leaders**
- **Platform:** Coursera (University of Minnesota)
- **Description:** This course teaches effective HR practices, staff recruitment, development, performance management, and creating a positive work environment in schools.

10. **Effective Communication for School Leaders**
- **Platform:** edX (Delft University of Technology)
- **Description:** This course enhances communication skills, including public speaking, interpersonal communication, and community engagement, which are crucial for school principals.

These courses provide a comprehensive foundation for aspiring and current school principals to develop leadership skills, manage school operations effectively, and foster a positive and productive educational environment.

About The Author

Dheeraj Mehrotra, MS, MPhil, PhD (Education Management)., a white and a yellow belt in SIX SIGMA, a

Certified NLP Business Diploma holder, is an Educational Innovator, Author, with expertise in Six Sigma In Education, Academic Audits, Neuro-Linguistic Programming (NLP), Total Quality Management In Education, an Experiential Educator, a CBSE Resource towards School Assessment (SQAA), CCE, JIT, Five S, and KAIZEN. He has authored over 100 books on computer science, AI, digital body language, NLP, quality circles, school management, classroom effectiveness, and safety and security. A former Principal at De Indian Public School, New Delhi, (INDIA), NPS International School, Guwahati, and Education Officer at GEMS, Gurgaon, with ample teaching experience of over Three Decades, he is a certified Trainer for Quality Circles/ TQM in Education and QCI Standards for School Accreditation/ School Audits and Management. He has also been honoured with the President of India's National Teacher Award in 2006 and the Best Science Teacher State Award (By the Ministry of Science and Technology, State of UP), Innovation in Education for his inception of Six Sigma In Education by Education Watch, New Delhi and Education World- Best Teacher Award, BOLT Learner Teacher Award by Air India, 'Innovation in Education Award 2016' by Higher Education Forum (HEF), Gujarat Chapter, among others. He has developed over 150 FREE EDUCATIONAL MOBILE Apps for the Google Play Store exclusively for Teachers, Students, and Parents. This work has been recognised by the LIMCA BOOK OF RECORDS and INDIA BOOK OF RECORDS as the only Indian to draw that feast. As a founder and president of the IoT Society of India, he also promotes Technology Globally. Dr Mehrotra is presently engaged as a PRINCIPAL at KUNWARS GLOBAL SCHOOL, Lucknow, India. He has conducted over 2000 workshops globally on "Excellence In Education" integrated with Total Quality Management and Six Sigma, Technology Integration in Education (TIE), Developing towards being ROCKSTAR TEACHERS, including Cyberspace, Cyber Security, Classroom Management, School Leadership & Management, and Innovative teaching within classrooms via Mind Maps, NLP and Experiential Learning in Academics. He is an active TEDx speaker and can be viewed on the YouTube TEDx channel. As a premium UDEMY Instructor, he has developed over 500 courses and caters to over 8 Lakh students from 180 countries. He can be visited at www.authordheerajmehrotra.com

Books By The Same Author

www.authordheerajmehrotra.com

Importance Of A School Principal

"*A principal plays a pivotal role in shaping a school's culture, guiding educational excellence, and fostering a supportive environment for students and staff. Their leadership ensures the effective implementation of educational policies, promotes continuous improvement, and inspires a shared vision of success within the school community.*"

"*A principal's importance lies in their ability to lead and inspire. They drive academic achievement, maintain school discipline, and nurture a positive learning environment. Their vision and leadership skills directly impact the school's culture, student outcomes, and overall success, making them essential to any educational institution.*"

www.ingramcontent.com/pod-product-compliance
Lightning Source LLC
Chambersburg PA
CBHW031458130726
47989CB00003B/1453